SAVING MONEY

By

C. Foster Stanback

Saving Money
Copyright © 2011
Foster Stanback
Cover design by Jonathan Stanback

All rights reserved. No part of the publication may be reproduced, stored in a retrieval system, or transmitted to any form or by any means—electronic, mechanical, photocopying, recording, or otherwise—without the prior written permission of the author and publisher. The only exception is brief quotations in printed or online reviews.

Published by Lulu®
www.lulu.com

Printed in the United States of America

ISBN-978-1-105-09904-5

Acknowledgements

In the late 1960s scientists at Stanford University conducted an experiment using nursery school children as their subjects. They placed a marshmallow in front of each child and stated that they were free to eat it, but if they could wait until the researcher returned, they could have two marshmallows. Most of the subjects began to squirm in their seats soon after the researcher left the room. In the end, only about thirty percent of them were able to successfully delay gratification and win the second marshmallow. Follow up with these children years later revealed that those who could resist their urge to eat the marshmallow performed better in school and had higher SAT scores. Though not undertaken as part of the study, it would certainly be reasonable to assume that, due to their ability to delay gratification, many of these children also had a greater proclivity toward saving.

In my own experience, I have known many people who seem to have been instinctive savers from an early age. One of them is my son Jonathan (age 16 at the time of writing). A number of years ago he was invited to go to Austria to play in an international soccer tournament. We gave him $500 for spending money and he returned with virtually all of it, minus about $40 that he spent on gifts for my wife and me and a few other people. The money was left in a savings account for him, where it remains to this day.

Alhough I have written this book, I am not an instinctive saver. I would not consider myself a profligate spender either. Perhaps I am just somewhere in the middle. I would probably have eaten the marshmallow had I participated in the Stanford experiments back in the 1960s. Natural savers will obviously have some advantages, but that does not mean that things are hopeless for the rest of us. Saving is a skill that can be learned and steadily improved upon.

I have been fortunate enough to be surrounded by many instinctive savers—my father, my brothers, my father-in-law, my brother-in-law, my wife, and my son. From their examples, I have been able to cull many of the principles that are elaborated upon in the pages that follow.

Table Of Contents

Chapter 1
Introduction
11

Chapter 2
Get Started
23

Chapter 3
Despise Debt
31

Chapter 4
Don't Gamble
37

Chapter 5
Track Expenses
43

Chapter 6
Stay Single Or Stay Married
47

Chapter 7
Have A Small Family
51

Chapter 8
Use It Until It Breaks, Then Fix It
57

Chapter 9
Buy It Used
67

Chapter 10
Stay Healthy
71

Chapter 11
Cancel Monthly Services
77

Chapter 12
Use Cellphones Only
For Emergencies
81

Chapter 13
Rent A Home
Instead Of Buying It
85

Chapter 14
Don't Make Loans
93

Chapter 15
Make Planned Rather
Than Spontaneous Gifts To Charity
97

Chapter 16
Conclusion
105

Appendix
A Sample Budget Worksheet
111

Chapter 1

Introduction

A man with a surplus can control circumstances, but a man without a surplus is controlled by them, and often he has no opportunity to exercise judgment.

– Harvey S. Firestone

In the summer of 2011, as many average Americans were still struggling to find work during the ongoing financial crisis, an article appeared in *USA Today* with the title "More credit card debt might be good for the economy."[1] The writer's malicious advice to bring out the credit cards and start spending again was incomprehensible, given the massive amount of debt that was already burdening so many households. But his recommendation was not designed to make his readers (or his nation) wealthy, since debt does just the opposite. Rather, it was

---

[1] Paul Davidson, "More credit card debt might be good for the economy," *USA Today*, 17 June 2011. 1 July 2011.
<http://m.usatoday.com/article/money/economy/48516336>

designed to generate more profits for the credit card companies and the businesses that could benefit from consumer sales. Perhaps he had been hired by them to write the article. To be a bit more charitable, maybe his goal was not to exploit people for the benefit of the credit card industry and retailers, but like so many others, he had bought into the bizarre idea that spending money can make a nation and its citizens rich.

Even the government, which is supposedly charged with the responsibility of looking after the public's wellbeing, has taken an active role in spreading this false notion. To make matters worse, it has enacted policies to entice people to spend rather than save. In 2009, as the country continued its plunge into the financial crisis, Congress enacted the "Cash for Clunkers" program to lure people into the purchase of new vehicles that would supposedly offer better gas mileage. In reality, the difference between the new cars and the older models that people were getting rid of was insignificant, amounting to just a few miles per gallon. The policy did nothing to move the country away from its profligate oil consumption. In spite of the shot in the arm it provided for Detroit, GM declared bankruptcy a few months later and had to receive a $50 billion bailout.

The government has also adopted less obvious policies to flush out peoples' savings. These schemes typically go unnoticed by the general public. Under the guise of the abstruse term "quantitative easing," the Federal Reserve has engaged in money printing activities with the stated objective of keeping interest rates low. Supposedly, this policy will encourage businesses to take out cheap loans to expand their operations and hire new employees. The unstated objective is that the low interest rates provided by savings accounts and bond funds will convince people that it's not worth it to save anyway, so they might as well spend their surplus income. As an added incentive, the inevitable inflation resulting from printing too much money will cause prices to rise so quickly that people will want to run out and buy things now rather than later.

Why so many of the nation's leaders and economists think that such policies can eventually lead to prosperity is a mystery. In the long run they cannot. Eventually, the nation and its people will pay a terrible price for following a pathway that defies all common sense. Though spending (especially with money that we don't have) might make us feel rich, the euphoria doesn't last long. It is soon followed by poverty and feelings of helplessness, anxiety, and despair. Debt, like its counterparts in the illegal drug world, only gives people a temporary fix. Then the dosage must be steadily increased to get the same high. Unless an addict can successfully kick the habit, he will usually end up in the gutter.

There is only one way to reverse the pervasive destruction caused by debt—stop spending and start saving. Unless you belong to a tribe of hunter-gatherers, it will be impossible to do this completely. Food, clothing, and shelter must be paid for with money in modern societies. But there are innumerable choices as to what we will eat, how we will dress, and where we will live. Most of us also have at least some discretionary expenses that we can opt out of.

If we can structure our lives to allow for the build up of a healthy surplus of funds, we will have the necessary cash reserves to avoid taking on debt even in emergencies. But even if we find ourselves buried under a pile of debt rather sitting on top of a pile of savings, it is never too late to start digging our way out.

There is no shortage of books and articles that offer guidelines and tips for saving money. Many of them have been written by people who whose proficiency in the art is truly astounding. Once someone is committed to making saving a priority, there will be abundant opportunities for learning and further development. Lifestyle changes may be dramatic at first, followed by a number of incremental improvements over the years. But none of this can happen without first coming to a profound realization that saving—not spending—will ultimately provide us with the rich and abundant life that we all desire.

Saving should not be an end in itself, but rather a means to an end. Money is a tool that we can use to store the proceeds from our labor. With this tool we can buy the things that we need, such as food and shelter, as well as the things that we enjoy. Problems emerge when we allocate too much of this money toward the things that we enjoy and our ability to provide for our needs becomes compromised. Adequately providing for necessities also means having some reserves so that in unforeseen circumstances, such as an accident or losing a job, we can still take care of ourselves.

Yet it is also important to spend freely to take care of legitimate needs. Nearly a hundred years ago Hetty Green, known as "the witch of Wall Street," became one of the richest women in American history. She was obsessed with money from an early age.

When she was only six years old, she used to tag along with her father, who owned a fleet of whaling ships, and read him the financial newspapers. At age 13 she became the bookkeeper for the family business and invested her earnings in the bond market.

Her excessive frugality and stinginess would become legendary. On her 21st birthday she refused to light the candles on her cake so that they wouldn't be wasted. The next day she cleaned them off and took them back to the store for a refund. Suspecting that potential suitors might only be interested in her money, she held off marriage until the age of 33. She finally wed Edward Henry Green, who came from a wealthy Vermont family, after he agreed to renounce all claims on her money. By that time, she had parlayed a fortune of $5 million inherited from her father into an even larger sum by investing in Civil War bonds. Hetty proved to be much more skilled in financial matters than her husband, and when she eventually had to pay off one of his debts, she dumped him.

In her later years she became more and more eccentric. She wore the same black dress day after day and only had the bottom washed to save money on soap. She would wear the same undergarments until they were worn out. Some accounts claim that she would eat oatmeal heated on top of the radiator in order to save fuel and that she would buy broken cookies in bulk. Another story claims that she spent half the night looking for a two-cent stamp.

When her son Ned dislocated his knee in a sledding accident, she took him to one of the free clinics for the poor. By that time her fame as one of the wealthiest women in America was widespread, and upon being recognized by the doctors she stormed away and vowed to treat her son's leg herself. Eventually, the leg had to be amputated. Ned later inherited his mother's $100 million fortune ($3 billion in today's dollars) and became a spendthrift, but it was probably little compensation for the lost leg.

Being frugal and saving does not mean we have to end up like Hetty Green. Just as a fuel efficient car can meet our transportation needs without wasting gas, a cash efficient lifestyle can still meet all of our needs without wasting money. Some people may indeed need to impose strict austerity measures upon themselves, but only for a time. Once debt has been eliminated and there is a steady flow of surplus funds into savings, relaxing the standards a bit to get more enjoyment out of life is fine. Maintaining a frugal lifestyle will not only allow us to keep building our cash reserves, it will also enable us to thoughtfully spend our money on the things we really enjoy, instead of wasting it on impulse purchases.

This book is not designed to provide an extensive list of practical ways to save money. Rather, it is intended to give support for the time honored principles of saving that have recently been assailed on so many fronts. With this goal in mind, attention has been brought to bear on some of the most significant ways we can reduce our spending, even when pointing them out may be offensive to some people. A meaningful discussion about saving must deal first and foremost with these "elephants in the room."

Chapter 2

Get Started

You cannot change your destination overnight, but you can change your direction overnight.

— Jim Rohn

Many people say they would like to start saving, but can't at the moment because they are living paycheck to paycheck. In many cases, it will take some time to implement the structural and lifestyle changes that will be necessary to free up any significant amount of cash for this purpose. When a person starts out with debt, it makes no sense to hold back money that could otherwise be used to pay off principal and reduce interest payments. But even when you owe a lot of money, setting aside at least a small amount on a regular basis is prudent, if for no other reason than to develop the right habit. Also, it is important to keep something in reserve for emergencies, such as an unforeseen medical expense. Sadly, many Americans have had to use credit cards to pay for healthcare costs, and end up saddled with high interest payments that gouge into the funds they need to live on.

A simple technique that anyone can implement right away (no matter what his or her financial circumstances are) is to save nickels. For a previous generation pennies would have worked, but inflation has so eroded their value that doing so would now be far too trivial even for a child. No doubt, many will scorn nickels as well, but for someone who really doesn't have any funds to spare, this is at least a start. Those in better circumstances can upgrade to silver or even gold coins, which they can purchase from a dealer. Even so, emptying your pockets and dropping a few nickels into a can at the end of each day doesn't do any harm—and the money can always be donated to charity in the end. This is a practice that can also be taught to children to reinforce the virtues of saving at an early age.

So why nickels rather than dimes or quarters? First of all, nickels represent less money that will be culled from daily living expenses—an important incentive for those who are truly in dire circumstances. Because of the smaller value of each coin, you may be less inclined to raid the hoard in a pinch. Secondly, the melt value of nickels is currently more than 7 cents. Nickels are made of nickel (no surprise) and copper. Both of these metals trade for a relatively high value on commodities exchanges. Like the silver coins that went out of circulation in 1965, there is certainly a possibility that these nickels could one day be sold to a coin dealer for more than their face value. A 50-cent roll of pre-1982 pennies (the year their copper content was drastically reduced) sells for around $1 today.

Some investors are willing to buy them in the hope that they can cash them in for their metal value when the price of copper goes up. Even if this happens, these investors will have to figure out how to get around the laws that prohibit the melting of U.S. coins, an offense that currently carries a penalty of up to five years in prison and up to $10,000 in fines. But the saver who simply pulls coins out of circulation will not have to worry about any of these details. He can just sell the accumulated hoard for a premium on eBay or to a dealer and let someone else solve the problem. Even if a market for "real" nickels never develops and you can't cash in on their metal value, you can still spend them or exchange them for some other savings instrument.

As available funds increase, a more elaborate savings plan can be developed that may include things like stocks. Even when you have passed the stage of saving nickels, which many people will decide to skip altogether, it is still good to hold onto some type of physical asset that is fairly liquid and transportable. Silver and gold coins are ideal for this purpose. Bank accounts can be frozen and liens can be placed on your home. If you are still in the process of digging out of debt and your assets are seized, you'll at least have something to fall back on. Even when you have achieved financial stability, identity theft or fraud can temporarily make it impossible to access your funds. A small business owner based in Missouri was a victim of credit card fraud in the amount of $30,000. The bank seized control of all the money in his business checking account pending a long investigation. He ended up having to pay all of his suppliers with personal savings or risk losing his company.

Even very wealthy people can be temporarily cut off from their paper assets. The owner of the Los Angeles Dodgers was worth nearly a billion dollars when he became involved in a messy divorce. The courts placed all of his assets under the control of a custodian until everything was settled, a process that was still pending at the time this book was being written. During an interview on public radio, he claimed that he didn't even have the power to write a check anymore.

Once you have set aside a moderate sum in tangible assets for a "worst case scenario," you can move on to more conventional vehicles like a savings or investment account. Starting early in life with a regular savings plan can make a drastic difference in the amount you will have available years down the road when it is time to retire. If you begin at age 25 and save $100 each month (and you are lucky enough to obtain a 5% return), you will have close to $200,000 when you reach the age of 70. If you wait until you are 45 to start saving, you will only have around $60,000 by age 70. Two hundred thousand dollars is a lot better than sixty thousand dollars, but neither amount will be enough to live on without working.

Anyone who wants to actually survive on the income from his or her investments will need to save a whole lot more for many years. Getting an early start is critical. If someone has a goal of accumulating $1 million to retire with (still not enough without working or a generous pension plan), a 25-year-old would need to set aside $450 per month for the rest of his working years until he reached the age of 70. A 45-year-old, on the other hand, would need to set aside $1700 per month until reaching 70 (a daunting task for someone earning a middle class salary averaging from $2000-4000 per month).

Chapter 3

Despise Debt

A creditor is worse than a slave owner; for the master owns only your person, but a creditor owns your dignity, and can command it.

– Victor Hugo

Debt is poison—period. Any form of it (whether it be credit card debt, a mortgage, or even a student loan) is bad. Some financial planners speak of good debt and bad debt, but it is all bad. It is like alcohol. This substance, when people consume it, is never good for the body. Even when alcohol is combined with antioxidant benefits, such as in a glass of red wine, it is converted to sugar and raises triglycerides. Yet when it is consumed in moderation, the health risks are probably minimal for most people. And so it is with debt. If it is consumed in moderation, it is usually possible to avoid severe damage from it's toxic effects. But like alcohol, it is terribly addictive, and some people should never touch it in any form whatsoever.

There are also some types of debt that are far more dangerous than others. Credit card debt is analogous to the pure alcohol often consumed by bums in the street. A student loan or primary mortgage is more like the occasional glass of beer or wine. Some people will be able to manage these less destructive forms of debt, but those who want to enjoy the greatest possible financial health will choose to avoid it altogether.

In the past, student loans seemed like a good idea for people who couldn't get scholarships and whose parents did not have the means to pay for their education. That was when there were plenty of jobs available and a college grad could quickly pay off the loans. Times have changed.

Consider Erik Soleki, who accumulated $185,000 in debt to obtain a Bachelor's degree in industrial engineering from Kettering University. After graduating, he was unemployed for nine months before he finally found a job that paid him $15,000 less than he anticipated. The new job did not offer him nearly enough to afford the $1800 monthly payments on his student loan. Even if he manages to scrounge together the money every month, it will take many years of living in austerity to pay the loan off.

Shane Dixon earned a Bachelor's degree in biology, but the best job he could find only paid him $7.25 per hour. After working for a year at that wage, he went back to school and obtained a Masters degree in public health. He finally found a low paying job working for the government in Florida, but he has little hope of ever paying off the $72,800 debt he has accumulated.

Michelle Shipley acquired a Bachelor's degree in political science and international development from Tulane University—and a student debt of $140,000. Her low wage job at a nonprofit offers little possibility of affording the $1400 monthly payments that will soon begin.[2]

---

[2] Annalyn Censky, "My Degree Isn't Worth The Debt," *CNN Money*, 11 July 2011. 13 July 2011. <http://finance.yahoo.com/college-education/article/113010/degree-not-worth-debt-cnnmoney%27%20rel=%27nofollow>.

The dilemma of these students is common today. Even when they have obtained difficult degrees in technical fields, the possibilities of finding a well paying job are slim, if they can even find a job at all! Some fields of study, especially the humanities and social sciences, offer very poor prospects of earning a living wage. The possibility of ever paying off all the debt incurred to obtain a degree in these fields is even more remote. This does not mean that you should avoid studying something you are passionate about.

Lynn Applegate, Chair of the Department of Sociology at Florida Atlantic University, has realized that the employment prospects for her graduates are rather bleak. She therefore encourages them to pursue a career in a trade, such as becoming a master electrician, so that they will still be able to pay the bills after they receive their university level education. Many such trades have good salaries and the jobs can't be exported overseas. Once a person has secured a decent salary, he can use part of it to pay tuition costs—an excellent investment!

Chapter 4

Don't Gamble

Every gambler knows that the secret to survivin'
Is knowin' what to throw away and knowing what to keep
'Cause every hand's a winner and every hand's a loser
And the best that you can hope for is to die in your sleep.

—Kenny Rogers

One of the surest ways to sink into the mire of debt is to gamble. In the past, society seemed to recognize the inherent danger of this vice. The federal government and most states had strict laws forbidding the practice. Of course, those who were determined could always find a way to get around the laws, but in general most people recognized gambling as something that was morally wrong.

Now, however, the betting "games" purveyed by casinos are simply viewed as harmless entertainment. States and municipalities are even getting in on the act. At first, they just sold lottery tickets, often with the pretext that the profits could be used to fund a worthy public cause like education. Sadly, the primary customers were poor and working class folk who would throw away their meager savings on a one in a million chance of hitting the jackpot. Sales of lottery tickets have increased dramatically since the beginning of the financial crisis in 2007. Growing numbers of desperate, out of work people are placing their hope in a lottery rather than in a methodical plan to lower their expenses, extricate themselves from debt, and accumulate savings.

The Internet made it possible for people to gamble without going to Vegas, Atlantic City, or an Indian reservation. Soon states wanted to tap into this lucrative business. By fleecing the poorest of their citizens, they could fill up the depleted state and municipal coffers. The ongoing financial crisis has given further impetus to this trend, and many state and local governments are currently trying to get around the Justice Department laws against Internet gambling. This lack of moral leadership by the institutions that are supposedly charged with looking after the wellbeing of their citizens is deplorable. Perhaps the next stage in the decline will be state run crack houses and brothels.

Many people will undoubtably recognize the foolishness of lotteries and casino games. But there are other forms of gambling that are less obvious. The stock market has always been a socially acceptable venue for gaming. Many of these games have been disguised as investments. Margin loans have traditionally been the fuel for speculation in the stock market. Prodded by brokerage firms that earn fat interest payments on the loans, investors hand over the stocks they own as collateral and are provided with easy cash to make bets on stocks they think are going to go up. Why be content with the meager returns from capital gains on stocks you actually own when it is possible to buy a lot more of the stock with borrowed money? To keep things interesting, you can also make a bet that the stock will go down by borrowing the stock itself from the brokerage firm, then selling it and buying the shares back once the price goes down. After returning the original number of shares that you borrowed to the brokerage firm, you get to pocket the cash left over in your account!

    These simple games are more like the slot machines in the Vegas casinos—just pull the handle and hope you get three apples. But the really "savvy" gamblers can play with derivatives, currency trading, commodities, etc. If you're bored, your broker will be happy to cook up something really interesting—and drinks will be on the house! It's all great fun until you lose your shirt and get kicked out of the casino with your tail between your legs. Savers should avoid the Wall Street gambling houses like the plague. When their local reps try to entice you or make you feel important with an invitation to play with the big boys, you should walk away and put your money in the bank. If you've done enough research to feel confident enough to buy stocks on your own, then you can buy them online with a discount brokerage firm.

Chapter 5

Track Expenses

The palest ink is better than the sharpest memory.

—Chinese proverb

As almost everyone knows, it is impossible to effectively manage your expenses and maximize the funds allocated to savings without a budget. Lots of people have at one time or another written down a master plan for how they want to spend their money. Unfortunately, in most cases the plan never gets implemented. The problem almost always results from a failure to track expenses. Like a daily exercise routine, this is the tedious and tiresome aspect of budgeting that often breaks down in the face of time pressure and hectic schedules. No one wants to tally up the day's expenses at eleven o'clock at night any more than they want to go jogging at this ungodly hour. And who wants to have to stop after every purchase and write down every single expense? But alas, this is the only way.

Modern technology has given us some wonderful tools that can make this task easier and even a bit more interesting. There are iPhone apps that will efficiently categorize and total up all of our expenses—as long as we take the time to input the data. Even our credit card purchases can be downloaded into computer programs, where they can be digested and processed into pie charts and graphs. As long as the downloads are performed on a regular basis and supplemented with data about purchases made with cash or checks, these programs are an excellent tool. For those who are uncomfortable with such technology—or who have shunned it as part of their budget plan—an old fashioned pencil and notepad can also work very well.

When all else fails, one of the simplest techniques to control spending is to take all the cash from your paycheck and divide it up into different envelopes that have been labeled according to the categories you want to manage in your budget (rent, food, utilities, gas, savings, etc.). Once the money from a particular envelope has been spent, that's it. As long as you don't put any new money in, adherence to your budget will be assured.

Chapter 6

Stay Single Or Stay Married

I'm an excellent housekeeper. Every time I get a divorce, I keep the house.

—Zsa Zsa Gabore

Even the best laid budget plans backed by rigorous discipline can be completely wrecked by a divorce. For a large segment of the population, the damage has already been done. You may have already lost half of your net worth to an ex-spouse and be struggling to make child support payments or pay the rent as a single mom. Many will no doubt feel that the price was well worth it to be rid of the jerk or the witch they were previously married to. But even those who are divorced will most likely choose to marry again at some point, and it will be important to avoid getting financially whacked all over again. So, if you are single and plan to marry, choose carefully or have a lawyer draw up a good prenuptial agreement.

Finding a spouse that appreciates the value of frugality and that is willing to live under the yoke of a budget will greatly improve the odds of having a successful marriage. Studies have shown that finances are one of the primary causes of matrimonial conflict. The other big one is sex, but that is an issue for a different book.

Chapter 7

Have A Small Family

There was an old woman who lived in a shoe.
She had so many children, she didn't know what to do.
She gave them some broth without any bread;
And whipped them all soundly and put them to bed.

—Mother Goose

Most people who get married want to eventually have children. And in most cultures the matter of how much it will cost to raise them is a question that simply shouldn't be asked. China, with its one child policy, is a well known exception. The government there has wisely realized that with a population of one billion people, any compromise could easily bring disaster upon the nation. From 1958-1961, a famine caused some 45 million people to die of starvation.

Unfortunately, many people in other nations fail to realize that having too many children can bring economic disaster upon their families. Perhaps they won't starve, but each new child causes a significant reduction in the standard of living for everyone else. In the past, having a large family was a matter of survival. Many infants died in childbirth and even those who lived often succumbed to disease within a few years. When most people lived on farms and produced their own food, another child meant another worker and perhaps greater prosperity. But in a modern urban setting, children are totally dependent upon their parents to provide for them until they leave the home and start working on their own. Every new addition to the family means that less money is available for food, clothing, schoolbooks, or vacations.

The U.S. Department of Agriculture has calculated the cost of raising a child in a middle class lifestyle from age one to eighteen at over $250,000. This number breaks down to nearly $1200 per month.

Most people never consider making such a calculation when they decide to have another child. Indeed, doing so would even be offensive to them. Other expenses can be evaluated in this way, but kids are off limits! Everyone can sacrifice a little bit and the money will somehow "stretch" to meet the need. But unlike a snake's mouth, which can stretch to swallow larger prey, money doesn't stretch to swallow larger expenses. A thousand dollars is a thousand dollars and one way or another it will be taken away from the other members of the family. Perhaps the sacrifice will be worth it, and that is for the parents to decide, but the cost and the lifestyle implications should at least be analyzed first. Doing so is not cold and heartless, but failing to do so really is, because it will have definite consequences for the wellbeing of any other children.

The author once knew a family of Mexican immigrants that was living in the Los Angeles area. Unlike many of their compatriots, the father had managed to procure a salary well above minimum wage.

The company he worked for paid him $15 per hour to place fresh flower arrangements in the homes of wealthy Angelinos and Hollywood moguls. This salary had so far been sufficient to support his wife and three children, in spite of some egregious financial blunders he had made. To transport his large family, he had purchased a brand new Ford Expedition SUV, which he failed to insure and promptly totaled in an accident. With large monthly payments going toward a nonexistent vehicle, he proceeded to buy a brand new car of the very same type. Now he had to make two car payments every month. In this precarious financial state, he decided to add yet another member to his already large family—his wife became pregnant with their fourth child. Sadly, this family now faced imminent economic collapse and the other children would have to bear much of the suffering.

Pets are also a wonderful addition to a family—if you can afford them. As with children, the Chinese government at one time imposed a strict policy on its people to look out for their best interests. For many years, pets were outlawed in the country. Some people raised dogs, but they typically ended up on the dinner plate. For Westerners, eating a dog would be unthinkable, and depriving people of the right to animal companionship is an outrage. But when people are very poor, the emotional satisfaction derived from a pet is an unaffordable luxury. Either the animal will suffer from inadequate food and veterinary care, or the family will suffer as money needed to live on is spent taking care of a pet.

In America the cost of having a dog has been calculated to be around $12000 over its entire lifespan—about $71 per month if the dog lives for 14 years and doesn't require any surgeries or other major veterinary expenses. If it does, then the cost could easily triple. For pet lovers, this expense will be worth it. But for those with limited budgets, other people will make much better (and less expensive) companions.

Chapter 8

Use It Until It Breaks, Then Fix It

Use it up, wear it out, make it do or do without.

– Unknown

Repairing things that are broken has almost become a lost art in our society. We are a throwaway culture. But the habits of the previous generation were very different from our own. A refrigerator would last nearly a lifetime. A television set might be replaced every ten years or so. Children grew up wearing hand-me-down clothes (often with patches sewn into them). Granted, one of the reasons we don't repair things anymore is that many of our products are much more complicated than they used to be. They often have electronic components that would be difficult if not impossible to fix ourselves. For many products, manufacturers don't even make replacement parts.

For items such as these, we may have no choice but to just go out and buy a new one when it breaks. Yet all too often, we are enamored by "newness" and eagerly dispose of fixable items so we can upgrade to the latest model. An important key to saving is to extract every last bit of utility from the products we use before throwing them away. Having an all-business mentality regarding our material goods will dramatically reduce our cost of living.

Businesses are primarily concerned about profits. If they are not, they will not survive for long. When an important piece of equipment fails, a good business owner will typically undertake a careful analysis to determine whether it is cheaper repair it or have it replaced. Utility is the only concern. The satisfaction of having something new doesn't factor in at all. For some items, a marketing concern may prevail, and the image created by having new equipment may directly impact profits. For example, patients may be more inclined to visit doctors and dentists that have new, state of the art machines.

But anything that will be used in the back room out of the public eye can suffice as long as it works. Most people tend to act like business owners when dealing with certain pieces of equipment that they have come to depend on. No one really cares how old or how ugly the air conditioning unit or water heater is as long as it works. But everything seems to change when it comes to cars, electronics, and clothes. People often decide to trade in older models for newer ones simply because they want to have something that looks new or has a few more bells and whistles. They are willing to pay a premium for a new item and accept an immediate depreciation in its value once they take it home with them. A new car will typically lose $2000 in value as soon as it is driven off the lot.

In the early years of the auto industry, Ford dominated the market with its ubiquitous Model T. Streamlined production techniques and a no frills design brought the cost of an automobile down so much that it was accessible to the average American worker. By 1924 the cost was just $300 ($3800 in 2011 dollars). Henry Ford was adamant that customers could "choose any color they wanted, as long as it was black." General Motors eventually leapfrogged Ford's market dominance by adding more features and styling to their cars. Alfred P. Sloan, a marketing genius who ran the company from 1923-1946, also figured out that if he changed the models every year, people would be inclined to constantly buy new cars. In his mind "what was good for General Motors was good for the country." Sloan's ideas have shaped government policymakers even in the present day. He also left a lasting impact on American culture, helping to establish consumerism as the driving force behind the nation's economy.

In retrospect, it turns out that what is good for General Motors is not good for the country, and it's not good for you either. Some people, such as real estate agents, may need a newer car because they must drive clients around and want to convey a more professional image. In such cases, the expense of continually upgrading to a new vehicle may influence overall income to some degree. Many others, however, want to have the image that a new car conveys even though it will have no bearing whatsoever on their paychecks. It is fine if they decide that the pleasure derived from driving around in a new car is worth it to them. But unless they are relatively well off, they should consider whether the temporary enjoyment they will have can compare with the longterm satisfaction and peace of mind that funds in reserve can provide. As long as a vehicle is mechanically reliable, making periodic repairs and extending its lifespan will free up a significant portion of discretionary income that can then be allocated to savings.

 The author's brother-in-law is a high school math teacher who lives in Anaheim, California. Seventeen years ago he purchased a small, Honda Civic car. Every week he would hand wash and wax the vehicle (saving the $20 that would be spent taking it to a carwash). He was meticulous about performing the required maintenance, most of which he did himself. When he lacked the skills or the tools, he took it to an inexpensive but reliable mechanic—never to the dealer. After more than 200,000 miles the car is beginning to show a few signs of age, but it is in remarkably good shape and runs just fine. The money saved by avoiding vehicle upgrades (and large interest payments) over a period of nearly two decades amounts to tens of thousands of dollars. Much of this money was channeled into paying off his mortgage, so that his condominium was completely paid for in half the time stated in his loan documents. He now has no interest payments of any kind, so that a large portion of his paycheck goes toward savings.

His approach to car ownership stands in sharp contrast to one of the janitors that worked at his school. This man had quite a long commute to get to work—he lived over an hour away. But he made the trip in style. He drove a customized monster truck with a massive 8-cylinder engine and giant off road tires. His gas expenditures every month were around $1000, which probably represented more than a third of his salary.

Television sets are another major expense for many people. Even poor homes in Third World countries typically have a large TV as a center piece. Sadly, they are often purchased on credit at exorbitant rates of interest. In Mexico poor families sometimes pay rates as high as 75 percent to obtain a TV set valued at just a few hundred dollars. To acquire the item immediately rather than having to save for it, families are often willing to put up their tiny cinderblock homes as collateral. If they manage to complete all the payments, they end up spending thousands of dollars for the TV instead of just a few hundred dollars. If they fail to make a payment on time, the store will immediately dispatch one of its many agents to harass them. If they still don't pay up, their tiny home is confiscated and they are put out onto the street. Fortunately, usury has not yet reached such a deplorable level in the United States. So far, the weapons of the loan sharks have been limited to lowering a person's credit rating, putting a lien on a home, or sending out repo man to take back a vehicle.

    Buying a TV set or any other electronics on credit should be avoided at all costs. Usually, the sacrifice will only involve putting up with a slightly less spectacular entertainment experience. Even if we have to live with a fuzzy picture (or no picture at all) for a while, we'll probably be OK in the long run. If our computer goes on the fritz and we can't access the Internet, it won't be the end of the world. In an emergency you can always access it for free at a public library.

Chapter 9

Buy It Used

An object in possession seldom retains the same charm that it had in pursuit.

– Pliny the Younger

Whenever it is absolutely necessary to purchase something, you can save an enormous amount of money if you buy it used. Retail stores typically mark up their merchandise by 100 percent. Most products are used for a time and then thrown away or sold for a fraction of their original cost at garage sales or online auctions. Needless to say, purchasing items in a used condition through these other venues can free up a considerable amount of money for saving. Let someone else have the satisfaction of acquiring an item in its new, pristine state (along with the discouragement and frustration of that first dent, scratch, or tear). You, on the other hand, can have the satisfaction of knowing that you have plenty of money available if you need it, along with every bit of the function that the original user got out of a product.

In their groundbreaking book, *The Millionaire Next Door*, Thomas Stanley and William Danko tell of the surprising insights they gleaned from interviewing numerous affluent people. Contrary to popular opinion, many of those who have substantial wealth don't display it in the form of expensive material goods. Instead, they have "balance sheet wealth"—large financial assets with little or no debt. To maintain this condition, they often purchase products that are used—furniture, cars, and even clothes. They don't compromise on quality, however, as well-made products typically give many years of service and provide good value for the money spent on them. The money these people save by buying things that are used is constantly channeled into the acquisition of more financial assets, making them richer and richer all the time.

The authors contrast this behavior with those who do not have balance sheet wealth. Some of them may appear to be quite rich on the surface. They may own businesses or have well paying jobs. They then make every effort to display their status with extravagant homes, clothing, jewelry, and cars. Often, these items are purchased with credit, since a large income makes it possible to afford all the payments. Yet if an outsider were to take a look at the total value of all their assets after subtracting all the debt, he would see that many of these people were not really wealthy after all.

Chapter 10

Stay Healthy

What can be added to the happiness of a man who is in health, out of debt, and has a clear conscience?

—Adam Smith

Healthcare costs typically consume a significant portion of the average person's budget. Even when someone is fortunate enough to have a good medical insurance policy—and many don't—the copays on anything beyond a simple office visit really add up. Then there is the cost of medicines. The pharmaceutical companies, like any other business enterprise, are interested in maximizing their profits. The lion's share of their R&D money is not channeled into developing medicines that will provide a one-time cure for some of the worst diseases. Antibiotics, which often achieve this goal, are not very profitable for these companies, so there is little incentive to put a lot of money into their development. The big profits come from treating peoples' ongoing ailments for which there is no real cure—things like heart disease, ulcers, and depression.

People who accumulate debt rather than savings are likely to suffer from all of these conditions, and the pharmaceutical companies will be able to cash in as these poor souls spend even more money that they don't have on expensive medications. There is, however, a simple and reliable way of avoiding much of this misery: decide to live a healthy lifestyle that centers on a good diet, exercise, and plenty of rest.

Some might protest that doing these things is impossible for people who don't have a lot of money. They can't afford to shop at Whole Foods, don't have time to go to the gym, and can't sleep much because they are working a double shift. This is indeed a valid point. Making healthy lifestyle changes in the midst of financial difficulties can seem daunting, but it can still be done. It will take a lot of discipline rather than a lot of money.

One of the areas in which this discipline will need to be applied relentlessly is diet.

As the ancient Greek physician Hippocrates said, "Let food be thy medicine." While many businesses are struggling to make sales in the ongoing economic crisis, the fast food industry is flourishing, serving up tasty and inexpensive concoctions of grease, sugar, and chemicals for people who cannot afford healthier fare. The Yum Corporation, which owns such fine eating establishments as Kentucky Fried Chicken (Yes, that's what KFC stands for), Taco Bell, and Pizza Hut, is currently lobbying the government to allow poor people to use food stamps at their restaurants. Food stamps are managed by the USDA's Supplemental Nutrition Assistance program. Although supplementing peoples' nutrition with grease may be cheap now, in the long run it will be very expensive, both for the government and for the unfortunate people who make it their dietary staple.

Healthy fare at restaurants will never be able to compete in price with the factory prepared products heated up at fast food joints. For those on a limited budget, the only way to maintain a healthy diet will be to eat at home. When at work, you'll probably need to revive the ancient practice of bringing a bag lunch with you.

Instead of paying a gym to allow you to exercise on their equipment, you can do it for free. Walking, running, sit ups, pushups, etc. are simple ways to stay in shape on a budget. For those who like team sports, there are plenty of leagues that can be joined for free or for a nominal fee. If you cancel your cable service, you can kill two birds with one stone. You will save on the monthly fees and you will probably be able to get to bed earlier because you won't get sucked in by a late night TV program.

Chapter 11

Cancel Monthly Services

Leeches are blood-sucking creatures with a wormlike appearance. You find them in the tropics and in temperate zones. You will certainly encounter them when swimming in infested waters or making expedient water crossings. You can find them when passing through swampy, tropical vegetation and bogs. You can also find them while cleaning food animals, such as turtles, found in fresh water. Leeches can crawl into small openings; therefore, avoid camping in their habitats when possible. Keep your trousers tucked in your boots. Check yourself frequently for leeches.

—U.S. Army Survival Manual

Businesses make profits by selling products or services to customers. Once a sale has been made, the business must then find a new customer or watch its profits decline. Alternatively, it can make a repeat sale to the same customer. Ideally, it can do both, so that profits will steadily grow as it expands into new markets while continuing to sell to the customers it has already won. Cell phone carriers therefore want to make it extremely difficult for you to cancel their service while at the same time making it extremely easy and appealing to sign up.

To ensure that the cash flows into their coffers without interruption, they typically want to set up an automatic payment plan that draws money from your checking account or credit card. That way, they are in control of their payments and the regular draw will remain out of sight and out of mind for most customers. The monthly service business model has proven to be so lucrative that more and more companies want to jump on the bandwagon. Many software companies, which used to make one time sales selling programs, now want to sell memberships that will grant access for a monthly or annual fee. Fitness clubs, travel services, home warranty and appliance repair services, discount clubs, etc. all want to do the same. If you are not careful, you can end up with lots of these companies latched onto your bank account like a hoard of leeches. They will continually suck out your economic lifeblood, leaving you financially weak and sick. The only solution is to burn off as many of them as you can, though a few, like the power and water companies, may remain stuck on you for life.

Chapter 12

Use Cellphones Only For Emergencies

Don't call us, we'll call you.

—Dorothy Kilgallen

One of the monthly drains on income that should be seriously reevaluated is cellphone service. Nowadays, virtually everyone, no matter what their age or economic status, carries a cellphone. Kids and unemployed adults alike have come to view the ability to talk or text over the airwaves as an inalienable right. The cellphone companies have profited handsomely from this modern cultural development.

Cell phones are indeed an amazing technology. In underdeveloped countries they have allowed people to obtain phone service when the cost of putting in land lines would have made it all but impossible for many years to come. Cell phones have also created business opportunities for poor people in isolated, rural areas. In India, for example, some women have been able to obtain micro-loans from nonprofit organizations that they then used to purchase cell phones. They were able start small businesses in their villages by offering people the opportunity to make calls for a small fee.

Many small business owners, in underdeveloped countries as well as in industrialized nations like the United States, are able to use their cell phones to make themselves more accessible to clients or customers. Cell phones are also a very useful tool to have in emergencies, such as when your car breaks down. The insurance it can provide is probably worth the minimum monthly fee to obtain service. A pre-paid phone is also a good option.

When used in these ways, a cell phone can be a valuable asset. All to often, however, people end up using these devices to have long, unnecessary conversations with family and friends. One of the more burdensome aspects of modern life is that we feel compelled to make ourselves available to anyone at any time with our cellphones. For many of us, not an hour goes by without receiving a phone call or text that interrupts our routine or face to face conversations we are engaged in. Many within the younger crowd even feel a bizarre urge to Twitter their mundane activities and whereabouts throughout the day.

If staying connected all day long provides more pleasure than stress, and you can afford the phone and data plan, then handing over a significant portion of your paycheck to the cell phone company every month may be worth it to you. But if you are trying to dig out of a financial hole, getting rid of this expensive device should be at the top of the list. If you want to keep a phone for emergencies, then you will need to act like a Hollywood movie producer and maintain a "don't call us, we'll call you" policy.

Chapter 13

Rent A Home Instead Of Buying It

A man builds a fine house; and now he has a master, and a task for life; he is to furnish, watch, show it, and keep it in repair, the rest of his days.

—Ralph Waldo Emerson

Home ownership, long considered to be an integral part of "The American Dream," has now become "The American Nightmare." Before the onset of the financial crisis, millions of people who could not afford to buy a home were given easy loans that they would eventually default on. Others, who may have had the means to purchase a modest house, upgraded to large mansions with all the amenities. Many even got into the business of flipping homes, sometimes buying a whole array of them on cheap credit, with the idea that they could flip them for an easy profit.

As the party revved up, a lot of homeowners became temporarily rich. Seeing their net worth increase by leaps and bounds, they decided to spend like there was no tomorrow, taking out home equity loans for new cars, electronics, clothes, and vacations. Sadly, the party ended in 2008 and millions of Americans are still suffering from the hangover. Most of the people who bought a home during that period of wretched excess are now underwater in their mortgages, forced to to make large monthly payments toward a property with a value that was assessed in a state of drunken euphoria. Some are simply walking away and declaring bankruptcy, leaving the banks and loan companies that gave them the money holding the bag.

The financial fiasco that has caused so much suffering calls for a reevaluation of the merits of home ownership. In the past, property values in many locations tended to go up modestly over the years, making a home seem like a reasonable place to put one's savings. Yet as a category of investments, or asset class, real estate has historically not performed as well as stocks or bonds. A renter who had channeled his or her savings into these other vehicles (and had left it there to accumulate dividends and interest income) would have attained a higher net worth than someone who had bought a home and used the savings to make payments on the mortgage. There have been exceptions, of course. People who were savvy enough or lucky enough to purchase a prime property in the path of the next stage of urban sprawl may have made a killing. Likewise, people who were foolish enough or unlucky enough to purchase a really lousy stock may have taken a bath.

Nevertheless, it can safely be said that in general, renting ends up being cheaper than buying, which allows more funds to be channeled into savings. The reason is obvious: renters do not have to pay for mortgage interest, property taxes, or major repairs. Landlords will certainly embed a portion of these costs into the rents they charge, but market rates usually do not allow them to do this completely. They end up eating much of the expense when there is a housing glut and there are lots of rental properties available. They also can't anticipate when an air conditioning unit or furnace will need replacing or when a pipe will burst and flood the living room floor. If they try to build these potential costs into the rent, they will usually price themselves out of the market.

A lot of people are frustrated because they think that their monthly rental payments are simply being thrown away, rather than being used to build equity in a home. Yet they often fail to grasp that the "monthly" cost of owning a home will be much larger, which will draw away funds that could otherwise be channeled into savings. Home ownership should therefore be thought of as a lifestyle decision rather than a financial decision. And for many people, it is a good one. The satisfaction and convenience of being in complete control of your living space and adapting it to your own needs certainly has value. As long as you can afford it (while continuing to channel funds toward savings on a regular basis), a decision based on lifestyle rather than financial considerations is valid. Yet those who cannot afford to buy a home should not fret—they are still following a prudent financial course and the longer they stay on it, the better off they will be.

Those who want to own a home and are in a financial position to do so should think of their purchase in terms of an expense for "shelter" rather than money that will be "invested." This perspective will lessen the danger of allocating a disproportionate amount of funds for living quarters. All too often, people justify buying large and expensive homes because they think they are investing the money rather than spending it.

Nick Martin learned this lesson the hard way. He now lives in a small, sparsely furnished tract home that he rents for $900 a month in McFarland, Kansas. He drives his 11-year-old SUV to his part-time job teaching winemaking at the local community college.

Sadly, Mr. Martin's frugal living is not by choice. Twelve years previously, he and his family resided in central California. One summer evening, they were all enjoying a nice dinner at home when a bank representative called, asking for wiring instructions so he could send $14 million into their bank account. The unexpected funds came from the sale of an advertising business founded by his father and run by his brother and brother-in-law.

The IRS took $4 million right off the top for taxes, then the Martins began their spending spree: several new cars (including an Aston Martin), a $175,000 horse, a $7000 mink coat, and houses. They bought a 3.5-acre camp on a lakefront in the Adirondack mountains of New York, where they began construction of a large summer home (complete with a three-story boathouse). Eventually, they sunk $5.3 million into the project. While the building was going on, they decided to move to England, where they bought another home. As their expatriate living expenses began spiraling out of control, they decided to move back to Vermont, where they purchased another house for $650,000. Renovations soon added another $600,000 to the total price. By the time the financial crisis hit, the Martins were already stretched to the limit. Property values quickly collapsed, along with the values of other bad investments they had made, and it was game over.[3]

---

[3] Geraldine Fabrikant, "Family's Fall From Affluence Is Swift and Hard," *The New York Times*, 25 November 2010. 16 September 2011.
<http://www.nytimes.com/2010/11/26/business/26fall.html>

Chapter 14

Don't Make Loans

The surest way to ruin a man who doesn't know how to handle money is to give him some.

– George Bernard Shaw

It is astonishing that some people who have accumulated savings through hard work and frugal living are then willing to cast away these funds into the hands of others who have flagrantly disregarded such a discipline. If you truly believe in the principles of saving, then "what's good for the goose is good for the gander." Making loans of any amount to other people will always cause them harm. By doing so, you will violate one of the most important principles guiding your own financial life—despising debt. If you despise it, you should teach others to despise it as well. Not doing so is nothing less than hypocrisy.

Furthermore, loans can ruin relationships. At minimum, they change their nature; at worst, they completely destroy them. Once someone owes you money and can't pay you (which is typically the case), there will be a constant tension that will create awkwardness and distance. You will begin to have feelings of resentment (even if you successfully repress them). The person with the debt will feel a sense of shame and want to avoid you. What may have once been a very open and spontaneous relationship will become clouded and strained by the unpaid debt hanging over it.

Adhering to a strict policy of refusing to give loans does not mean you have to be calloused and stingy. You can always make a gift to a person who is truly in need. If he or she happens to be a friend or relative, a gift will not adversely affect the relationship like a loan will. Most likely, you will not make a gift that constitutes an enormous sum of money, so it will not destroy your budget. People who make loans are often duped into believing that even though a sum is extremely large, it will all be coming back to them. The sad truth is that all too often, the money disappears forever. People whose circumstances are so desperate that they resort to requesting money from family or friends are usually never able to implement the radical lifestyle changes necessary to generate enough surplus funds to pay you back.

Your savings should remain completely off limits when considering making a monetary gift. That way, you will never compromise the financial security that you have worked so hard to attain. Taking a portion of the monthly funds you use to live on will limit the size of the gift and make it much more meaningful, since you will truly feel the impact of your sacrifice.

Chapter 15

Make Planned Rather Than Spontaneous Gifts To Charity

Each man should give what he has decided in his heart to give, not reluctantly or under compulsion, for God loves a cheerful giver.

—The Apostle Paul (2 Corinthians 9:7 NIV)

If you are currently in a deep financial hole and are struggling even to pay the rent and buy groceries, gifts to charity will not be an option. In extreme cases you may even need to be a recipient of charitable gifts rather than a benefactor. If you are really in need and making every effort to work hard and live frugally, there is no shame in accepting help from other people. Hopefully, the experience will make you want to return the favor when circumstances are better.

Yet the natural progression of industriousness and frugality will lead to surpluses, even if you have to make a slow crawl for many years. At some point you will achieve financial stability and have a solid base of savings to which you regularly contribute. When it is within your means, giving something back to society or to those who are less fortunate is a virtue that is universally esteemed. Stinginess and greed, on the other hand, are despised in every culture of the world.

If your goal in life is to become the next Mother Teresa, you can live a life of poverty and give away everything to the poor except what you need for bare subsistence. Throughout history there have been many examples of noble individuals who dedicated themselves to a life of service at a cost of great material deprivation. However, this type of lifestyle is not for everyone, nor is it expected of everyone, regardless of the culture you belong to or the religious belief system you ascribe to.

What is expected is to be generous to the best of your ability, and it is certainly possible to embrace this virtue while still enjoying many of the pleasures that are available in this life. Some of these pleasures will be free, but others will cost money. There is nothing wrong with setting aside funds for a vacation or buying something we would like to have simply because we will enjoy it (once we have the means to do so without taking on debt). If we plan well and stick to our budgets, it should also be possible to set aside a certain amount to give to charity. The key, however, is planning.

All too often, gifts to charity are made spontaneously when we become moved emotionally by a plea from an individual or a nonprofit organization. To make matters worse, the dominant emotion that moves us is often guilt. Sometimes it is a sense of guilt for what we have that others do not. This is the absolute worst reason for making a charitable contribution. Spontaneous, guilt-driven giving robs us of the emotional reward we should naturally receive for being generous and frequently directs funds to ill-conceived programs for making the world a better place.

A common tactic employed by some nonprofits is to stand in front of shopping centers and grocery stores and ask passersby for donations. Busy shoppers often make an effort to avoid these interruptions by keeping as much distance as possible and avoiding eye contact. To thwart this tactic, petitioners typically call out in a loud voice, "Hello Sir, How are you today?" They then proceed with their pitch, "Would you like to help the homeless, earthquake victims, cancer victims, etc.?" Once a shopper has been engaged and made eye contact, he or she often succumbs to the request. Sometimes they acquiesce because they just want to get on their way without being impolite. Other times, they may feel a sense of guilt because they are entering a store that sells expensive merchandise and the person sitting at the table is just asking for a small donation to help the hungry.

    The problem with making a cash gift on the spot is that you usually don't know anything about the organization that the petitioner represents. It may just be a sham operation to make money. Even if the organization is legitimate, there is no way to tell whether the solicitor is an honest person, and there is no way to know whether your cash gift will be channeled into the said worthy cause or pocketed and used for booze or drugs. If you are in a poor country and a beggar who is blind or has no legs asks you for money, you can at least know that a bit of change will help that particular individual. However, you cannot know this when an obviously healthy representative of an organization claims that he will give your money to a needy person on your behalf.

Therefore, making spontaneous cash gifts to unknown solicitors is unwise. If you want to be polite when they call out to you, just tell them that you never make cash contributions on the spot, but that you will be happy to research their organization to see if it fits with your overall charitable giving goals. If you are in a hurry and the person wants to spend time explaining things to you, just tell him that you have to go and will need to take a card or flyer with you. After you have had adequate time to inform yourself about the organization, you can always make a direct gift by check so that there will be greater assurance that the money is going where it's supposed to go.

Giving away money intelligently is perhaps even more difficult than making it in the first place. Wise charitable gifts will involve a certain amount of calculus. Spontaneity, though wonderful when it comes to romance, is a vice when it comes to finances. Careful planning is the only way to maintain a state of balance and remain in the game for the long run (which will most likely result in a greater amount that is ultimately given to charitable causes).

Chapter 16
Conclusion

To preserve our independence, we must not let our rulers load us with perpetual debt. If we run into such debts, we must be taxed in our meat and drink, in our necessities and in our comforts, in our labor and in our amusements. If we can prevent the government from wasting the labor of the people, under the pretense of caring for them, they will be happy.

—Thomas Jefferson

As this conclusion is being written, government leaders in the United States reached a last minute agreement to avoid defaulting on the nation's debt. After months of squabbling, Democrats and Republicans agreed to a compromise that would allow for a temporary increase in the debt ceiling in exchange for spending cuts. Just like an individual who has borrowed too much money, the country has ended up between a rock and a hard place. Taking on more debt only makes things worse down the road when the money has to finally be paid back.

It is like getting a new credit card and using it to make payments on the credit cards you already have.

On the other hand, defaulting would have meant missing payments to people and institutions that the government owed money to, such as bondholders and civil service workers. Just like a homeowner who fails to make a mortgage payment on time, a missed check from the government means a lower credit rating and higher interest charges in the future. This, in turn, means that a greater percentage of tax revenues will have to be spent on interest instead of services for the American people.

Even though Congress finally agreed to raise the debt ceiling, one of the major rating agencies lowered the country's credit rating anyway. In their opinion, the national debt was spiraling out of control and the political will to fix the problem was lacking. Most policy makers acknowledge that spending will have to be curtailed at some point in the future, but many of them don't want to do it now. They believe that if the government borrows money and creates jobs with it by hiring people to work in state run programs, these people will spend the money they earn on consumer goods. Businesses will sell more products and start hiring new employees. Prosperity will magically return. No one seems to ask what will happen once the government stops paying people to work.

If countries could create prosperity by borrowing money and spending it, then Bangladesh could lift its citizens out of poverty by starting an Apollo program to go to the moon. A flawed policy that can't work for a poor nation won't work for a rich nation either, any more than it will work for an individual. The only true pathway to prosperity—for nations and the individuals that comprise them—is saving and investing.

Nations will need to refrain from fruitless wars and frivolous gifts designed to appease political constituencies. They will need to invest the proceeds from taxes into educating their citizens, building the infrastructure to facilitate business ventures, and protecting the natural resources that they depend on for survival.

Individuals will need to refrain from foolish purchases to appease their whims or impress their neighbors. They will need to channel surplus funds into safe savings instruments that they can rely upon in retirement or times of need. Ultimately, the economic strength of any nation will be derived from the financial strength of its citizens.

Winston Churchill once said that "Americans can always be counted on to do the right thing, after they have tried everything else." We have tried the pathway of profligate spending and it has brought us to the brink of economic destruction. Now, every citizen owes it to himself and to his country to make a radical course correction that will eventually lead to financial stability. Once the people of this great nation have renounced unbridled spending and debt in their own lives, they will no longer tolerate leaders who encourage these vices as a matter of public policy.

A Sample Budget Worksheet

The following worksheet provides a simple way to plan for monthly expenses and keep track of them. The column on the left has spaces to list different sources of income as well as various categories of expenses. When the total expenses exceed the total income, spending cuts will be necessary. Whenever you have an expense during the day, you should write it down and categorize it on a small notepad. At the end of the month, you can write the totals for each expense category in the right hand column of the budget worksheet to see how you well you followed your plan. This simple format can be easily adapted to include additional sources of income and different categories of expenses. Once you have created your own worksheet, you will have the ability to get a quick snapshot of how you are spending your money and where you can make cuts to allocate more to savings.

MONTHLY BUDGET
Month of _____

ANTICIPATED INCOME   **ACTUAL INCOME**

Salary _____   Salary _____

Other   _____   Other   _____

TOTAL   _____   TOTAL   _____

ANTICIPATED EXPENSES   **ACTUAL EXPENSES**

Basics   **Basics**

Rent/Mortgage _____   Rent/Mortgage _____

Food   _____   Food   _____

Utilities   **Utilities**

Water   _____   Water   _____

Electricity _____   Electricity _____

Gas   _____   Gas   _____

Communication   **Communication**

Telephone _____   Telephone _____

Cell Phone _____   Cell Phone _____

Cable TV	_____	Cable TV	_____
Internet	_____	Internet	_____

Transportation | | **Transportation** |

Car payment	_____	Car payment	_____
Gas	_____	Gas	_____
Insurance	_____	Insurance	_____
Main./Repairs	_____	Main./Repairs	_____
Bus/Metro/Taxi	_____	Bus/Metro/Taxi	_____

Healthcare | | **Healthcare** |

Insurance	_____	Insurance	_____
Doctor	_____	Doctor	_____
Dentist	_____	Dentist	_____
Medicine	_____	Medicine	_____

Personal | | **Personal** |

Toiletries	_____	Toiletries	_____
Clothing	_____	Clothing	_____
Haircuts	_____	Haircuts	_____

Gifts

Charity _____

Monetary Gifts _____

Presents _____

TOTAL _____

**SURPLUS/
DEFICIT** _____

Gifts

Charity _____

Monetary Gifts _____

Presents _____

TOTAL _____

**SURPLUS/
DEFICIT** _____

About The Author

Foster Stanback is a managing partner at various domestic and international firms engaged in business activities that include shipping, distribution, retail sales, and real estate. He has been an active investor in international equities markets for over two decades. He holds an M.A. in Sociology from Florida Atlantic University, where he received a distinguished alumnus award in 2011. He also holds an M.A. in Religion from Pepperdine University, an M.A. in Psychology from the Pepperdine Graduate School of Education and Psychology, and an M.S. in Marketing and Technology Innovation from the Worcester Polytechnic Institute. In 2010 he was inducted into the Beta Gamma Sigma International Honor Society for Collegiate Schools of Business.

www.ingramcontent.com/pod-product-compliance
Lightning Source LLC
Chambersburg PA
CBHW072214170526
45158CB00002BA/603